MW01491538

Father Joe Sica, son of the late Joseph J. Sica

Jr. and Elveria Rossi Sica, was born in Scranton on November 27, 1955. He received his early education at William Prescott #38 and graduated from Bishop O'Hara High School, Dunmore. As a seminary student, Father graduated from the University of Scranton, while in formation at St. Pius X, Dalton, and earned an M.A. degree from the Catholic University Theological College, Washington, D.C. Father Sica was ordained to the priesthood on April 24, 1982, by Bishop J. Carroll McCormick, D.D., late Bishop of Scranton.

Father Sica served various assignments in his nearly 38 years as a priest in the Diocese of Scranton. He served as

Detail of a portrait of Fr. Joe Sica, painted by Doria Mahoney and now hanging in the main vestibule of Immaculate Conception Church, Scranton, Pennsylvania.

(PHOTO COURTESY OF FR. PAT MCLAUGHLIN.)

assistant pastor of Annunciation Parish, Williamsport; Mount Carmel Parish, Carbondale; Our Lady of Snows Parish, Clarks Summit; St. Aloysius Parish, Wilkes-Barre; St. Mary's Parish, Scranton; and St. Peter's Cathedral, Scranton. He served as director of religious formation at Pocono Central Catholic High School, Cresco; Bishop O'Hara High School, Dunmore; and Bishop Hannan High School, Scranton. Father Sica served as pastor of Nativity B.V.M. Parish, Tunkhannock; and Holy Rosary Parish, Scranton; and as senior priest at Immaculate Conception Parish, Scranton. In addition, Father Sica served faithfully as a chaplain at Mercy Hospital in both Wilkes-Barre and Scranton. He will long be remembered for his pastoral outreach to the sick and suffering.

Father Sica was well known as an inspiring author. His books include *Embracing Change* and *Forgiveness: One Step at a Time*. In addition, for many years he published daily devotional booklets for Lent.

YOUR GUIDE
TO A
Happy
Life

Wisdom from
FR. JOE SICA

**TWENTY-THIRD
PUBLICATIONS**
twentythirdpublications.com

Twenty-Third Publications
One Montauk Avenue, Suite 200
New London, CT 06320
(860) 437-3012 or (800) 321-0411
www.twentythirdpublications.com

Cover photo courtesy of the Diocese of Scranton.

ISBN: 978-1-62785-564-8
Printed in the U.S.A.

 A division of Bayard, Inc.

CONTENTS

FOREWORD

On March 31, 2020, we lost a precious friend.

In a blink, he was gone…

But is he?

His desk was left perfectly clean; not a paper or pen misplaced. But sitting in front of us was the completed version of his 2021 Lenten reflections, ready to teach us once again. Ready to inspire us once again. Ready to give us hope once again.

Then silently in the background was another gift from Fr. Sica…. Another book, one none of us knew about, and just about ready to be published: *Your Guide to a Happy Life: Wisdom from Fr. Joe Sica*. This a collection of some of Fr. Sica's most treasured pieces that he left for us as a final gift.

For those of us who knew and loved him, our world is a darker place. Our job to honor him is to go forward with the faith and optimism of Fr. Joe Sica.

For those who did not know him, my hope is that this little book gives you a glimpse of who he was: a man who loved his work, loved his people, and loved his God.

His approach was often unconventional, and he was not saintly. But neither are most saints. And he lived by one basic principle: "What would Jesus do now?"

As Bishop Joseph Bambera beautifully described at Fr. Joe's graveside, "Every bishop should have a Joe Sica….Despite the occasional insanity, he baptized every baby, married every couple, and buried every person who sought a Catholic service. While so many of us were examining the rules, Joe Sica went to work welcoming so many into the arms of the Catholic faith." Yes, he acted as Jesus would want.

Wisdom is defined as "the natural ability to understand things that most people cannot understand." Wisdom can be packaged in many ways. There was only one package for Fr. Sica's wisdom. Perhaps unconventional, but it worked. This book, so appropriately titled, offers us a sample of his wisdom.

May you read these pages and smile, remembering the man he was.

So, to answer the original question… Is he really gone?

Not a chance; he's right here, still teaching….

He often said, "Remember, yesterday was in the past. Tomorrow is not yet here. So, really what we have is NOW." So go and live Life, now…. And enjoy the ride.

Fr. Joseph Sica, thank you for giving us this one last gift.

See you on the Other Side!

> With loving respect,
> Your friend,
> *Linda Barrasse*

PART I

Cultivate Joy

*"I have told you
this so that my joy
may be in you,
and your joy may
be complete."*

JOHN 15:11

Joyology

Dear Lord, use me to spread joy
and make my joy complete. Amen.

"**W**HAT GETS YOU THROUGH IT?" I ask, acknowledging someone's deep pain. "Splashes of joy," they respond, refreshed and ready to keep going. This is the key to the way we should live—simply and completely.

Grounded in God as the foundation of all our joy, we align our actions, interactions, choices, and behaviors with a joyous attitude and gratitude. We can become joyologists.

Attitude. Things often don't go according to plan. Sometimes they go utterly and spectacularly wrong. Joyologists aren't free of life's speed bumps. Life even delivers them a truckload of lemons on occasion. But joyologists simply edit out the negative, recognizing that negativity breeds negativity. Then they edit in the good that is happening, no matter how little or much.

Gratitude. Joyologists don't worry obsessively, lament over the might-have-beens, or get caught up in "someday...." They are grateful for every moment, give thanks for the good in their lives, and appreciate the little things—a breathtaking sunset, an engaging conversation, a delicious meal. Fully engaged in the now, when life gets bumpy, they choose to power ahead.

God directs joyologists to connect with people who are having a hard time bouncing back, helping them turn the lemons into a refreshing glass of lemonade.

HAPPINESS HABIT » *If you're feeling lost and unsure, list the things in life that bring you joy and happiness. Then go and enjoy them!*

Heaps of Healing Humor

*Jesus, help me believe that laughter makes life
the merriest of go-arounds. Amen.*

I WAS INSPIRED BY A WOMAN IN HER FOURTH STAGE OF OVARI-
AN CANCER. Even her doctors were amazed at how well she was
doing. Her secret? Laughter.

"My sense of humor helps me find a lighter side of things, even
on tough days," she told me.

What do we need to survive life's heartaches? Heaps of healing
humor. Healing humor reduces stress, elevates moods, boosts
the immune system, and fosters relaxation. It helps us overlook
the ugly, tolerate the unpleasant, cope with surprises, and smile
through the unbearable. Humor is a shock absorber, minimizing
the pain troubles can bring.

Today's people seem to be serious about everything. Some go
through life with their finger on the panic button, crossing bridges
before they get to them, certain trouble is just around the corner.
The prescription for those suffering from humor-deficiency: an
injection of laugher.

People with positive outlooks laugh often to relieve themselves
of life's tears. A good belly laugh stirs the blood, expands the chest,
and clears the cobwebs from the brain.

Laughter is a gift we need to survive. If it's missing, put it back!

HAPPINESS HABIT » *Schedule a "laughter-noon" with friends.
This could be an in-person visit or virtual visit through your computers
or mobile phones. The most important part? Share a laugh!*

Seize Life Daily

Jesus, you are so very good to give me
a fresh, bright, gift-wrapped day. Amen.

I LOVE THE SIGN ON THE DESK OF A FUNERAL DIRECTOR I KNOW: *ANY DAY ABOVE THE GROUND IS A GOOD ONE!* Look at each day with fresh eyes. Nobody has messed it up yet; it's a new day to enjoy. It's a day that hasn't been lived in, and you can live it with gusto.

How do we grab the gusto? How do we bring excitement into this life? I don't mean cheap, amusement-park-stimulated excitement. What can make us eager to leap out of bed in the morning, filled with purpose?

You'll find the secret on a bumper sticker that says *Carpe Diem—Seize the Day.* The phrase implies immediacy, passion, gusto. Hesitate and it's gone forever. Jesus advises John's disciples: Seize life! Don't let it go. Be ready to live it now, before it's too late.

We can't live our lives over, but we can make progress from where we are to where God wants us to be. Seize the day! Live every God-given moment. Enjoy life. Love those in your life and treat others with respect. Be remembered for your smile, the laugh lines around your eyes, and the twinkle deep within. Make every day special.

HAPPINESS HABIT » *Write Carpe Diem on index cards. Decorate them. Hand them out to family and friends.*

You Are Someone's Spotlight

Jesus, there's nothing more uplifting than knowing someone cared enough about me to influence me so well. Amen.

POP STAR DEMI LOVATO TOLD *COSMOPOLITAN* MAGAZINE, "When I was younger, I needed someone in the spotlight to idolize, who stood for positivity and light and happiness and wanted to change the world. And because I didn't have that, I realized I wanted to do that, if only for my twelve-year-old little sister."

Each of us carries the flu—not the disease kind, but the in-"flu"-ential kind. We will affect every person we come into contact with. Even if we're unaware, people will adopt certain mannerisms, catchphrases, and attitudes from us.

You're always communicating simply by being who you are, saying what you say, and doing what you do. You may be the only carrier of positive influence to another person.

When you're a healthy carrier of influence, you showcase absolute integrity, possess a positive frame of mind and attitude, deliberately listen, understand, and appreciate people's differences, and do what's right. You emphasize optimism, empathy, encouragement, and inspiration. The results? You experience a higher quality of life as you are healthier and feel good about yourself.

HAPPINESS HABIT » *Draw a circle on paper and write: "My sphere of influence." Whom could you influence in a positive and powerful way?*

Fortified Boundaries

Dear Lord, sometimes I go over the limit for others and I feel drained.
Encourage me to claim time for myself. Amen.

"TOURING ISN'T SOMETHING I'M GOOD AT," ADELE TOLD THE CROWD AT AUCKLAND'S MT. SMART STADIUM. "I don't know if I will ever tour again."

Boundaries are created when we understand and know what our personal limits are. When we try to do everything, we crash. Ultimately, we're stressed, pressed, sad, impatient, tired, and even angry; we feel weak and ashamed. To avoid going over the edge, we must recognize our boundaries and make the world comfortable for ourselves—while striving to be our absolute best within our comfort zone. Knowing our boundaries means downsizing, making healthy choices, or saying, "No, I can't do it."

We must also set healthy boundaries in our relationships by standing up for ourselves and refusing to tolerate pushy people or rude comments. Fortified boundaries preserve our integrity as we take responsibility for who we are by letting others know we have self-respect and won't tolerate having someone else define us. We are in the driver's seat of our lives.

HAPPINESS HABIT » *Give yourself permission to put you first. Choose a "Me Day." Go to a coffee shop, order a latte, and read a novel uninterrupted. Or come up with something uniquely you.*

Laughter: The Best Medicine

Jesus, help me to laugh at myself;
then I'll never cease to be amused. Amen.

T OO OFTEN WE TAKE OURSELVES TOO SERIOUSLY. We always worry about looking good and appearing dignified. The result is that we miss out on a lot of fun.

Laughter is nutrition for the soul, a tourniquet to stop a bleeding broken heart, a tonic for the discouraged. Things will inevitably happen that cause you to feel you've lost control. Yet, if you turn them around and laugh about them, circumstances will not control you. Laughing together over life's twists and turns is a great way to let off steam and keep stress to a minimum. When you do, you are in charge, instead of circumstances being in charge of you.

I once officiated at a wedding where I wanted everything to go off without a hitch. Just as I finished the opening prayer, the air conditioner kicked on from the vent above me. The air blasted my notes all over the wedding party. Paper hung in the air for one dramatic second before raining down and gliding under the pews. I cracked a joke, which broke the tension into hysterical laughter. Instead of being embarrassed or fretting over this "hitch," it became a happy, humorous memory.

HAPPINESS HABIT » *Give a mirror to someone who has forgotten how to laugh and remind them that life is like a mirror. If we frown at it, it frowns back. If we smile, it returns the greeting.*

Happiness at Work

Jesus, help me to create happiness in my life through patient and deliberate effort. Amen.

WHY SHOULDN'T OUR LIVES BE FULL OF BRIGHTNESS, GOODNESS, PRODUCTIVITY, AND GROWTH? We must hope that every decision we make, every action we perform, will take us in the right direction—the direction necessary for happiness. Even our mistakes can be cause for optimism by offering us opportunities for learning and greater awareness.

Happiness is difficult to define. It's a personal thing. For some, it is rare and only brought on by extraordinary circumstances. I, on the other hand, am most happy with ordinary things: dinner with friends, ministering at a hospital bed, a walk in the neighborhood, good conversation, a hug. Since each of us is unique, what makes one person happy may have the opposite effect upon another.

If we want happiness to be more than an irregular and passing feeling, then we must make a sound and strong commitment to make our own happiness. Abraham Lincoln said, "People are about as happy as they choose to be." Knowing that we're in the position to conjure up and shape our own happiness is precious knowledge. From there we can learn to bring into our lives the things that make us happy and keep them there, rather than wait for irregular visits.

HAPPINESS HABIT » *Collect as many memories of happiness as you can. Keep them in a journal or in a file on your computer. Encourage your children to start their own journals. They will serve as a reservoir of strength when the clouds roll in, when you're wallowing in misery, or whenever you need it the most.*

The Spice of Life

Jesus, create a desire in me to understand others
without rushing to conclusions. Amen.

It's sometimes very easy to lose your cool with loved ones. In anger, we try to correct their faults, question their decisions, and challenge their views. But if we truly desire what is best for them, we have to abandon anger.

Anger is a complex, subtle emotion, not to be taken up lightly. Sometimes anger can be good. When we're treated unfairly, anger can be the motivator we need to help us stand up for ourselves. But the next time we're tempted to speak from anger and say, "The trouble with you is," hold that thought.

Anger must be tamed. When you approach your boiling point, take a deep breath and slowly repeat a word or phrase like "take it easy" or "relax." Replace your critical thoughts with positive and rational ones. Once you're calm, speak to the person(s) involved about whatever is frustrating you. Share your feelings and perceptions, rather than blaming others or assuming you know what's going on with them. Listen to what the other person says. Take a time-out before responding.

In order to live a joyful, balanced life with healthy relationships, we must manage our anger rather than destroy another person.

HAPPINESS HABIT » *Make "Anger Tamers" sticky notes with phrases like "Count to ten"; "Jesus, help me"; "Be still." Place them in visible locations in your home—the refrigerator, the bathroom mirror, the computer screen, the television. Look at them whenever you feel you're about to explode.*

Tag! You're It!

Jesus, I want to live simply now and then,
putting aside the complexities of life. Amen.

W HEN IS THE LAST TIME YOU JUMPED IN A PILE OF LEAVES OR PLAYED A GAME OF HIDE-AND-SEEK? Have you gathered an armful of lilacs lately? Grown a milk mustache? While I'm not suggesting you avoid grown-up responsibilities, I am recommending that you take off your adult mask and act like a child again. By doing so, you tap into your own personal fountain of youth.

We can't always escape the bad times in life—there's suffering, sorrow, and pain—but we can decide to give ourselves an occasional sabbatical from hurt. On this day, stress and problems are prohibited. Begin the day by tendering your resignation from adulthood and engaging in a few childlike activities.

Be impulsive and adventurous! Embrace simple blessings that often go unnoticed—snowflakes falling or leaves changing color. Look for ways to enjoy life's simple pleasures. The evening's moonlight. A crackling fire. Go to the park and feed the ducks. Treat yourself to a Happy Meal and a shake.

As a child, in the absence of competitiveness and worry, we knew only joy. We believed in the power of smiles, hugs, kindness...and making snow angels.

At the end of your "hurt-break" day, congratulate yourself. Phone a friend and share some special thoughts. Enjoy life's taken-for-granted delights. There sure are plenty of them.

HAPPINESS HABIT » *Make the first day of every month a hurt-break day. Open only good mail and purposefully do something enjoyable.*

Don't Worry, Be Happy

*Dear Jesus, it's time to open my heart, let go of the worry,
and trust that you'll help me when I ask. Amen.*

M ANY OF US BELIEVE THAT WORRYING ABOUT SOMETHING
IS NOT GOING TO CHANGE THE OUTCOME. One gentleman,
however, doesn't agree. He was lying on the couch talking to his therapist and said, "Worrying works for me. Ninety-nine percent of the
things I worry about never happen."

If you're like me, you too probably believe this—worry about it,
and it won't happen. Whenever something unexpected occurs, we
tend to start worrying about the worst possible scenario.

Wouldn't it be nice if we could take all of our worries and just not
worry about them anymore—just be happy? We can.

When life hits us and so many things can go wrong, the remedy
is not to worry yourself sick, but relinquish worry through prayer.

Pray about what's really in your heart. Pray about everything (no
exceptions). In other words, there is no problem, no circumstance,
and no situation that cannot be brought before God.

Accept the invitation of Jesus to "ask," and then trust Jesus will
fill your need or mend your hurt. Prayer is a meaningful conversation with God. Ask for guidance. Request to be led to the perfect
person who can help you!

HAPPINESS HABIT » *Friends can give you a different perspective,
but there's a caveat here: be sure you pick people who have control over
their own worries. Find someone who can listen and offer positive and
constructive support.*

Choose Carefully

Jesus, there's nothing more uplifting than knowing someone cared about me enough to set a good example for me to follow. Amen.

R OLE MODELS ENABLE AND ENCOURAGE US TO BECOME THE PERSON WE WANT TO BE. Too many people think role models have to be famous—sports figures, actors, or musicians. But real role models tend to be parents, teachers, or coaches. They're the ones who guide us on our life's journey.

We need to surround ourselves with role models who are a joy to be with. Their positive and enriching presence in our lives nurtures and encourages us to be the best we can be. They motivate us to achieve our dreams, inspire us to uncover our true potential, offer constructive advice, empower us to overcome obstacles, and prompt necessary changes.

Our role models are not intimidated by our success, because they know there's an unlimited amount of it to go around. The wrong role models can drag us down. They lure us toward unhealthy behaviors that can hurt our lives. It matters whom you emulate. Choose carefully.

HAPPINESS HABIT » *"Like always attracts like." In order to keep yourself surrounded by positive role models, stay happy and positive and watch the people you'll attract into your life. Send a note of appreciation and gratitude to your role models!*

PART 2

Heal the Hurt

"I have heard your prayer; I have seen your tears. Now I am healing you."

2 KINGS 20:5

The Healing Power of Tears

Jesus, thank you for the gift of tears. They're your
way of not letting my heart burst. Amen.

A FOUR-YEAR-OLD BOY HAD GONE NEXT DOOR TO VISIT A RECENTLY WIDOWED GENTLEMAN. "What did you say to him?" asked his mother. "Nothing, Mommy," he replied. "I just climbed onto his lap, rested my head against his chest, and helped him to cry."

Often, we carry muted sorrows, covering them with a pretense of "everything is fine." We hold back the tears to keep them from surfacing. Living wounds are buried alive.

It's unsettling to lower the drawbridge and invite people in to see the hurt in our hearts.

Broken people often say to me, "I'm sorry. I didn't mean to cry. Please excuse me." I tell them there's no need to hold back the tears; I encourage them to let them flow. Then I hand them a tissue.

Benedict Carey refers to tears as "emotional perspiration." Crying, lamenting, sobbing, and wailing…they make us feel free and cleansed. We get it all out like a good workout sweat. When we're crying, our feelings go unchecked. We're vulnerable and able to connect at a deeper level. Crying sends us down the path toward healing.

HAPPINESS HABIT » *Find a safe place to shed your tears.*

Cancel Your Guilt Trip

Jesus, with your help, guilt has worn out its welcome in my life.
Fresh starts are happening. Amen.

M ATTHEW BOOKED HIMSELF ON A GUILT TRIP. "I missed my brother's birthday. I should have at least phoned. Now it's too late and I look like a fool." Matthew could have cut his guilt trip short by saying, "I missed my brother's birthday, but I'm going to send him a card and apologize." Guilt doesn't want us to think about how we can avoid repeating the same mistake. Guilt keeps us spinning our wheels in mud rather than finding ways to change.

We become our own deejays and keep spinning records in our minds that make us miserable. We all have our top ten lists of songs tormenting us as they pop into our minds: "I shouldn't have waited so long to reach out to him," or "I made such a fool of myself over something petty," or "I wish I'd gone to see her in the hospital. Now she's dead." When we keep pressing the Play and Repeat buttons, we internalize bad messages. We see ourselves through a distorted lens.

But we're in control of the Guilt Play List. How much airtime are we going to give it? Cancel the guilt trip and book a different one: I'm sorry, and I'm changing. Switching from guilt to this after doing something regrettable says, "I goofed. Give me a chance to make it right."

HAPPINESS HABIT » *Talk with someone you trust about the guilt feelings that are permanent residents in your life. Use Jeremiah 31:34; 1 John 1:9; Hebrews 10:22; and Romans 6:18 as your guilt-zappers.*

Face Life Fearlessly

Jesus, with your help I can
handle any fear. Amen.

WITH HEART POUNDING AND KNEES KNOCKING, MARY WOR-RIED ABOUT HAVING A BABY. Although panic, apprehension, and hesitation raced through her mind, the angel calmed her and eliminated doubts about her pregnancy, allowing her to overcome her fears.

We can't let our lives be ruled by fear or we'll enjoy very few experiences. So it's time to face your fears and forget about them; time to change your "What if…?" thinking into "I can handle this with God's guidance!" thinking.

Look fear in the eye and ask yourself two questions: "What's the worst thing that can happen?" and "How will I deal with it?" Write down positive steps you can take to face your fears. Be realistic, but believe that, with God's help, you have the strength to handle anything. Then let it go and move ahead. Repeat these practices, and you'll find your self-confidence rising to high levels.

HAPPINESS HABIT » *On a "Fear Management Scale," where would you rate yourself? Are you a 1—"I'm often paralyzed by fear"? or a 10—"I almost never let fear stop me"? What would you like your score to be? Listen to God's most repeated command in Scripture: Fear not. That sentence is repeated over 350 times in the Bible. There must be a reason!*

Tune Out the Chronic Critics

Jesus, thank you for never giving up on me, or walking away from me, or leaving me at the mercy of the chronic critics. Amen.

THE LIFE OF THE WOMAN CAUGHT IN THE ACT OF ADULTERY WOULD NEVER BE THE SAME, not because of the stones of condemnation ready to be thrown by her critics, but because of the compassionate words of forgiveness spoken to her by Jesus, a reliable rescuer.

We've all experienced an abundance of criticism regarding our dress, our talk, or our thinking. Chronic critics can make us feel shame, guilt, and incompetence—if we let them.

Stop listening to them. Listen to reliable rescuers who push us to change, learn, grow, and discover in new and better ways.

Reliable rescuers endorse our self-worth and cherish us as holy, unrepeatable persons fashioned in the image and likeness of God, blessed with abundant possibilities. They encourage us to believe that who we are today is not who we'll be tomorrow. If we've messed up, they don't judge or condemn but give us chances to put our mistakes and failures behind us and start over, reminding us that no condition is permanent.

Kick chronic critics out of your life. If you continue to give them a voice, you will fail to hear God's gentle whisper, "Become who you are: special, beautiful, unique, lovable, and capable."

HAPPINESS HABIT » *Instead of dwelling on chronic critics, focus on your gifts, talents, and strengths. Pay attention to reliable rescuers who turn your life around. Read Philippians 4:6–9.*

Resurrection Recovery

*Jesus, help me to recover with resurrection power when life
knocks me down, and to help others do the same. Amen.*

W HY DID GOD LET THIS HAPPEN? WHEN IS ENOUGH GOING TO
BE ENOUGH? HOW MUCH MORE DO I HAVE TO TAKE? I'm often
asked these questions, and I wish I had the answers. When we're reeling from shock, we can either fall into despair or we can recover with
resurrection power.

Jesus has been there. Just look at the week before his crucifixion. It starts out with a throng of followers singing his praises as
he enters Jerusalem. In a matter of days, the crowd's cheers turn to
jeers. An associate sells him out for a few coins. Other supposedly
loyal friends can't even stay awake when he needs their support. And
his prized disciple says, "I don't know him"—not once but three
times.

Like Jesus, we've been through the wringer. We've walked
through fire. We've experienced heartbreaks. But through the
pain, something good has happened. Jesus has fine-tuned us with
resurrection power, able to ascend from shocks and unanswered
questions, able to look hurt in the face, turn it inside out, and learn
from it. We make the adjustments needed and move on. We are
changed. Our heartbreaks make us more compassionate, more
caring, more loving, and more aware of another's pain.

HAPPINESS HABIT » *Give erasers to people who are in the midst
of a heartbreak. It's to remind them Jesus will erase what has happened,
slowly and gently.*

No Unheard Cries

Jesus, I believe you hear my cries when I am damaged and hurt. Amen.

J ANUARY 10, 2003—12:47 AM. One moment I was anticipating my mom's recovery from open heart surgery, and the next I learned she was in the presence of God. Afterward, driving with my sister to her house, I kept hearing the doctor's voice, "Father, I did all I could. You mom's heart was too weak. I'm sorry." Crawling into bed, I thought, "This must be a bad dream." But it wasn't. Our mom was dead.

The next day, my sister received a package marked "Damaged in transit but deliverable." The string was hanging, the label missing, and books stuck out of one corner. Generally, I wouldn't have given the "damaged" label a second thought, but the day it arrived my heart was broken. That package connected to my hurt. Jesus knew I needed something to remind me that there are things in life I can't do anything about. Jesus says, "I know you've been damaged in transit, but don't stop there. Read the rest: 'still deliverable.'"

We journey at our own paces, from "damaged" to "deliverable." Our journeys will be easier if we remain open to the things that connect to our hurt. For me, it was: a package label; a movie starring Angelina Jolie, *Life or Something Like It*, gently reminding that time and people are precious; a sermon by Brother Edward, urging me to turn my hurt over to God; a song by Celine Dion, "My Heart Will Go On"—especially the line, "Every night in my dreams, I see you. I feel you. That is how I know you go on." I refuse to let life's tragedies define me and destroy me. By which reminders will your journey be defined?

HAPPINESS HABIT » *When troubles damage you in transit, make a list of everything you can't do anything about, and acknowledge that Jesus can. Post it on your bathroom mirror. Add items as necessary.*

Misery Is Optional

Jesus, teach me lessons from your desert duel with the devil.
And when life gets tough, help me to keep moving forward. Amen.

L IFE CAN BE MESSY AT TIMES. Loss, illness, accidents, and tragedies muddy the water. Suffering isn't fun. In fact, it can be
awful.

Author Tim Hansel reminds us that "pain is inevitable, but
misery is optional." The difference between winning and losing is
how we react to life's hurts. What we do with our pain can be more
important than the pain itself. Whining crowds our hearts with bitterness. Rehearsing the details invites sadness. We can opt out of life
for a while, but eventually we'll need to make the conscious choice
to move on, taking baby steps toward living again.

Often, it takes a huge effort to get moving. But after we're all
cried out and the anger has mellowed, we know it's time to open
the door and step out into the world once more.

It's not easy. It takes determination and strength to let go, engage
in conversations, accept invitations, or simply pull back the covers
from our beds. But we're a part of this world, and each day that we
spend hidden away only prevents us from the opportunity to live
fully.

HAPPINESS HABIT » *Pause for a minute and think about life like a cup
of water. When it's full, there's no room for anything else. As life continues
to present new opportunities, it will consistently overflow because your cup
is always full. You have to pour out those unhappy moments from the cup
so there will be room for new things in life.*

Being Wrong Happily Ever After

Jesus, I take responsibility for all the wrongs I've said or done.
I sincerely desire to grow and change from these experiences. Amen.

"I MIGHT BE WRONG." Don't you love hearing those magic words? Have you ever said them? How about, "You might be right"? These powerful phrases can unlock wondrous things in our relationships.

God doesn't expect us always to be right. Nor does he expect us to be another's judge, like the Pharisee who felt he needed no improvement and looked down at the tax collector. When we free ourselves from the need to be right all the time, we're free to learn from others.

I've learned to live with being wrong happily ever after. It has taught me humility. And in the process, it has released me from the illusion of perfection. I was raised on "Try again," and discovered my successes were often in direct proportion to my persistence, not to being right.

Having the courage to say, "I'm wrong," shows strength and character. It's far better than always trying to present yourself as flawless and perfect. Besides, what does it profit you if you're always right and you win each argument, but in the process you've lost a friend?

HAPPINESS HABIT » *Take a deep breath, close your eyes, and whisper, "I was wrong." Try looking in the mirror and saying it when no one is around. It's refreshing to admit we're flawed, a reminder that our shortcomings, once acknowledged, become opportunities for growth and healing.*

Let It Out and Let It Go

Jesus, thank you for the gift of prayer.
Forgive me for neglecting it. Amen.

J OANNE SAT AT HER DAUGHTER'S BEDSIDE IN HOSPICE. Two years earlier, she'd lost her oldest daughter to the same kind of cancer. As she held back tears, I asked Joanne how she was doing.

"Can I be completely honest with you, Father?"

"Absolutely."

"Am I the problem? Is Jesus listening? Do my prayers matter?" Desperation filled her eyes as she looked to me for an answer.

Pretending we don't feel despair or hopelessness is living a life of denial. When we act as if nothing is wrong, we can fool our friends and family, but we can't fool Jesus. He's waiting for us to pour out our hearts to him.

Genuine prayer expresses drudgery as well as inspiration, fear as well as joy, doubt as well as faith. The relief combination is sob and surrender. Go to Jesus, pour out your feelings, and let them explode from the depths of your brokenness. Don't hold back. God gives us tears to drain the abscesses of our deepest pain. And remember, you're in good company. Even Jesus wept when his heart was broken.

All done crying? Now give it to Jesus. He's our most intimate friend. Watch what happens after you feel heard and, most importantly, loved.

HAPPINESS HABIT » *Seal your troubles in an envelope. Get on your knees, lift up the envelope with both hands, and tell Jesus your troubles. As tears flow, drop your arms and say, "Jesus, take it."*

Enough!

*Jesus, give me the courage to stand up to all
the critics and say, "Enough!" Amen.*

I ONCE KNEW A WOMAN WHO HAD JUST ABOUT EVERYTHING A PERSON COULD WANT. She was beautiful, well-educated, wealthy, and generous.

But even with all her fine qualities, she was miserable. At times, she was so deeply depressed that she contemplated ending her life. How did she get into that sad state? By listening to the comments of critical people. She lived in fear that if she didn't measure up to their expectations, she wouldn't be loved.

Finally, weary of being held back and of the constant need for approval, she found the courage to stand up for herself. "Enough!" she said. "I'm tired of doing and being what others expect of me. Just to fit in, I'm missing out on the beauty of being me, with my own ideas and desires."

Critical people are all around us. My preferred approach to them comes from Mario Andretti. When asked for his number-one tip for success in race car driving, he said, "Don't look at the wall. Your car goes where your eyes go." Your mind will go where your attention is focused. Negative comments stir up anger and self-doubt. Focus on them and you'll run right into the wall. Instead, focus on moving ahead with your dreams and aspirations. Ignore the boos. They usually come from the cheap seats anyway.

HAPPINESS HABIT » *Critical people need love too! The next time someone criticizes you, simply respond with a compliment and see what happens.*

One Is the Loneliest Number

Jesus, thank you for continually connecting with,
and never forgetting about, me. Amen.

T HEIR MARRIAGE WAS IN TROUBLE, SO THE COUPLE WENT TO
SEE A THERAPIST. After about thirty minutes, the therapist got
up and gave the wife a big hug. He said to her husband, "Your wife
needs this every day." The husband responded, "Okay, Doctor. But I
can only bring her in here every Monday and Thursday."

When we stop and think about what we live for and what matters most, we usually think of a person—a spouse, child, parent, or
friend.

To thrive and survive, we need warmhearted contact with other
people. We're born with an insatiable need for meaningful connec-
tions with others. It begins the first day of our lives and continues
until we take our last breath.

Building the relationships we desire—making them more intimate and fun—helps complete us as people. We're at our best when
we're connected in working relationships with others, and at our
worst when we're disconnected. Without feeling connected, we
can't grow into a fully human being.

To conquer loneliness, we must have significant loving people in
our lives. We need to work to consciously package our strengths so
we can deliver clear, compelling invitations to the people who will
complete us.

HAPPINESS HABIT » *Feeling lonely may be an indication that you
need to discover ways to renew relationships. Devise plans for spending time
with family and friends. Connect with people you haven't heard
from in a while.*

PART 3

Change Perspective

*"Have among yourselves
the same attitude
that is also yours
in Christ Jesus..."*

PHILIPPIANS 2:5

"Aha!" Changes Everything

*Jesus, I will always cherish those special moments
that opened up unlimited possibilities for me to love. Amen.*

"THERE'S NOTHING BETTER THAN WHEN SOMETHING COMES AND HITS YOU AND YOU THINK 'YES!'" says author J.K. Rowling. Once you do, the world's all different.

Life has a way of getting our attention through Mountain Top Experiences. These experiences provide plenty of "aha!" moments where we have instant clarity. Everything makes sense and motivates change in us as we charge forward. It's a lightbulb moment, and time stops. Ideas and feelings flood our souls with understanding, and we finally "get it."

Don't let those "aha!" moments go to waste. Act on them. Let them inspire you to make lasting changes.

A man told me his recent heart attack was his "aha!" moment. Now he's spending more time with his family, especially his grandson. The health scare was an eye-opener for him as he realized how quickly he could have been gone. Now he's made significant changes in the way he's doing things. Suddenly, what used to take priority in his life seems trivial. "My heart attack," he said, "gave me a new lease on life and I'm not going to miss it." Aha! moments. "Bam!" A great fog is lifted, and we gain a newer and wiser perspective on life.

HAPPINESS HABIT » *Talk with a trusted friend about your aha! moments and how they changed you.*

Sneer or Cheer

Jesus, today I made a grand discovery:
that you believe in me and my dreams. Amen.

A T OUR SCHOOL'S SPRING ART SHOW, EVERYONE MARVELED
AT CHRIS. He could paint, draw, and sculpt beautifully. His
dream was to have an exhibit at New York's Metropolitan Museum
of Art, but he worried about family and friends' perception of artists.

One day Chris told me he was finally ready to take his life seriously. "For years," he admitted, "I've wanted to study art, but I've been
afraid of the fallout from family and friends. I pushed that dream
deep down and have remained a 'good boy' ever since. But I have
talent, and I refuse to hide that part of me any longer."

When we decide to stretch beyond our comfort zones and follow
our dreams, we'll probably hear from dream-sneerers, saying things
like: "Who do you think you are?" Why allow dream-sneerers to
spoil our dreams? Let's kick them out of our lives and welcome
dream-cheerers, people who inspire us to discover our potential.

When Jesus said, "Follow me," some mocked his choice of disciples. Fishermen? Tax collectors? "Get real. You sell fish," the
dream-sneerers snarled. But these people refused to listen and chose
to follow Jesus, a dream-cheerer who radiated encouragement.

Once we stop caring what dream-sneerers think about us and
begin caring about who we are becoming, the dream-sneerers will
disappear, and the dream-cheerers will appear.

HAPPINESS HABIT » *Spend time today allowing God to direct your
dream potential to develop. You're never too old to dream of new things.
Begin by listing three dreams, even if they seem impossible.*

Born to Bounce Back

Jesus, every now and then life will throw a punch at me. The more I roll with these punches, the easier it is to bounce back! Help me to roll with them. Amen.

L IFE GOES ON. The first time I really understood this was the morning after my father died. I opened my eyes to see another beautiful spring day. Clearly, the earth had turned in the night. The sun was shining. Birds were singing. People were talking in the street. I couldn't believe it, but it was true. Life goes on.

In the face of disappointment, disaster, or grief, life goes on, whether we go on or not. Setbacks come in all shapes and sizes and we don't always handle them with ease. Divorce, bankruptcy, cancer, or the death of a loved one—these events have the capacity to crush us forever. They can also redirect us toward the people and things that matter most. So how do we find that gift of really living after experiencing such setbacks?

Tap into God's healing power! It gives us the ability to get back up after we've been knocked off our feet. When life throws us a devastating punch, we must express our feelings, deal with our anger or sadness, and face our fears. Once we're in touch with these feelings, with God's help, we can work on releasing them.

Setbacks bring us lessons about life and relationships. If we learn the lesson, we can bounce back and experience stronger personal relationships, clarity about our priorities, and greater personal strength. Then we can find a deeper appreciation for life and emerge from the experience feeling totally alive.

HAPPINESS HABIT » *Start the day with this bold affirmation: "Go ahead, Life, send me a setback. I eat setbacks for breakfast; they are my fuel for the day!"*

Empty Spaces

Jesus, give me the energy and motivation
to simplify my life. Amen.

"EMPTY SPACES," MY FRIEND ARLENE EXPLAINED WHEN I ASKED HER WHAT SHE COLLECTS. Her husband, on the other hand, fills their home to the brim with antique furniture, action figures, comic books, and his prize collection of little metal cars and trucks. There are literally thousands of them.

Relatives of mine have their wedding-day Waterford crystal and Lenox china neatly packed in the original boxes, complete with the beautiful white ribbons. They aren't even sure why they're saving them.

The fact of the matter is, we love our stuff. If it doesn't wear out, we store it. For what?

What effect does having all this stuff have on us? We should follow Arlene's lead: Collecting "empty spaces" will surely help us feel lighter and healthier the minute we start. And, of course, we can start right now. By sorting and sifting through all of the stuff in our boxes, drawers, closets, attics, basements, and garages, we can streamline our lives.

When you pick something up, make a decision about it. Realize you can either have that or the empty space. Donate your usable items to charity and give someone else the opportunity to enjoy them. Simplifying is one of the healthiest things you can do. You'll be amazed at how peaceful your life can be once you start a new collection of empty spaces.

HAPPINESS HABIT » *Make your home a relaxing, enjoyable place to live. Set up a relaxation room by keeping the strict minimum in it. Create an empty space and there talk to God.*

Change Your Attitude

Jesus, help me to never look down on anyone—
except for the purpose of helping them up. Amen.

ONE DAY A MOTHER HEARD A SCREAM FROM THE ROOM WHERE HER THREE-YEAR-OLD SON AND ONE-YEAR-OLD DAUGHTER WERE PLAYING. Her son tearfully related that his sister had pulled his hair. Mom explained that it really wasn't his sister's intention to hurt him; she just didn't know any better.

Mom returned to her work but, within a couple of minutes, heard another scream; this time from her daughter. Hardly looking up from his toys, her son quietly said, "Now she knows."

Many of us—maybe most of us—know how it feels to be judged incorrectly. We know how deeply it can hurt. It should also mean we know not to do it to others.

In two words, blunt and absolute, Jesus commands us: "Stop judging." Jesus is talking about putting people down when we think they're wrong, rather than finding ways to build them up. This judgmental attitude hurts us and makes us feel inadequate.

A regular diet of judging shuts down possibilities and smothers the insights of our hearts. Judging prevents us from seeing the goodness that lies below the surface and beyond the appearance.

We can choose to become the people we want to judge; we can step into their circumstances and try to see the world through their eyes. This view may change our attitude completely.

HAPPINESS HABIT » *Try living one day judgment-free. Have an open mind with no requirements, conditions, or expectations.*

Hot under the Collar

Jesus, don't let my anger control me
before I confront the situation. Amen.

W E'VE ALL FELT ANGER AND RESENTMENT. Let me suggest
three steps to manage anger when someone or something
triggers your anger switch:

Create and Cool. Give yourself a time-out to create space
where you can be alone. A prayer closet is an ideal place to
let hot thoughts cool down. Take time to truly reflect on the
situation.

Cause and Check. What's causing your anger? Is someone
being treated unfairly? Are people trampling all over your
rights? Are you trying to right a wrong? Did someone intrude
on your privacy? Check out your feelings: Do you feel threat-
ened, anxious, or simply irritated?

Concentrate and Consider. Use a double column to make a list
of the helps and hurts of feeling angry and reacting with a "get
even" attitude. Write down the short- and long-term consequences of your anger and whether these consequences are
acceptable or unacceptable. Consider creative solutions to
correct the difficulties.

HAPPINESS HABIT » *Make a sign that says, "Count to Ten"*
(or some other reminder to stay cool). Place it in a visible location in your
home. Then attempt reconciliation in a situation in which your anger
damaged your relationship with someone.

The Elephant in the Room

Jesus, through the power of your love, I'm breaking loose.
There's so much I don't want to miss in my life. Amen.

A MAN STOPPED IN FRONT OF THE ELEPHANTS, confused that the huge animals were being held by only a small rope tied to their front legs. No chains, no cages. They surely could break away from their bonds, but inexplicably, they didn't.

He asked the trainer why.

"Well," the trainer said, "when they're very young and much smaller, we use the same size rope to tie them. At that age, it's enough to hold them. As they grow, they're conditioned to believe they cannot break away, so they never try."

Like the elephants, we're bound by a small rope of outdated behaviors, thoughts, beliefs, or reactions. As a result, we keep doing what we've always done and end up with the same results.

Two words hold us hostage: "What if?" What if I fail, get fired, mocked, or rejected? So what? Try. It may be scary, but with each step you'll build confidence. Cut loose and see what happens. We tend to stop short of trying something different. Instead of taking a chance, we are passively bound by self-imposed ropes.

Whenever you want, you can decide to cut the rope and reach toward your highest potential. You're bound only by your attitude. It's up to you to move forward and leave the past behind.

HAPPINESS HABIT » *What ropes do you need to cut?*
Make a list of everything that holds you back and cut loose.

On Second Thought

Jesus, forgive me for the times I have been quick to judge others before discovering rich opportunities to grow closer to them. Amen.

W HEN THE HAPPY COUPLE EXCHANGED WEDDING VOWS, Maria's family and friends thought, "What does she possibly see in him?" Nathan had massive arms covered with tattoos. He rode a motorcycle and wore the usual biker attire. Maria was completely turned off by him at first. It was only after she got to know him that she discovered his gentleness and kindness. He was someone she wanted to spend the rest of her life with.

Judgments: we make them quickly, without thinking. We don't have to love everyone we meet or be friends with everyone, but we should give them a chance. We are too quick to judge others by the way they dress, their hairstyles, their jobs, their ages, or any number of reasons that keep us from seeing, hearing, or appreciating them.

Try viewing people through judgment-free glasses. We may find that people like Cousin Alice, who's considered a bore, or our neighbor, who's deemed aloof, are suddenly rather likable people. It's not that they've changed; it's we who have changed our minds about them.

HAPPINESS HABIT » *Give yourself a judgment-free day. Practice understanding, compassion, and acceptance. Pay a compliment. Then extend it to a judgment-free week, month, and year. This exercise will help change your attitude completely.*

Crazy Busy Is Simply Crazy

Dear Jesus, I don't want to look back on my life and say, "I wish…"
Help me cherish my family and give them the time they deserve now. Amen.

A COMMON RESPONSE TO "HOW ARE YOU?" THESE DAYS IS A RESOUNDING, "CRAZY BUSY." When we're racing from one activity to another, quality family time dissolves. But in the end, it's all about family. They're the ones who catch you when you fall, guide you when you're lost, and revive hope when you feel like giving up.

At the end of life, you won't regret not responding to every email or text, but you may wish you hadn't missed the opportunities to spend time with those you love. When life seems busier than ever, it's time to hop off the treadmill and work harder at making your family a priority.

Don't know where to begin? Start small. Have dinner together and share stories of the day. Dust off the board games. Take a walk, jump rope, or play tag. Enjoy a movie, concert, or sporting event together. Create memories. Spending more time together may be a challenge at first, but soon it will become a family routine everyone will look forward to.

HAPPINESS HABIT » *The possibilities are endless. Plan a family night. Ride bikes together. Schedule an arts and crafts activity. Read a story. It doesn't have to be a major project. All it requires is time together.*

It's Time for Some Easy Listening

Jesus, help me curb the urge to give advice
when I'm only asked to listen. Amen.

B ATTLING SEVERE DEPRESSION, MY FRIEND'S DAUGHTER TRIED
TO COMMUNICATE HER STRUGGLE TO HER PARENTS. As she
repeatedly told them her world was caving in around her, they chose,
for whatever reason, not to hear her, even when she told them she'd
considered suicide. Fortunately, she failed at her attempt at suicide
sometime later. Her parents were dumbstruck. "Why didn't you tell
us you were hurting and having problems?" they asked.

Instead of engaging our ears, we engage our mouths. We have our
own agenda and opinions. Often, we interrupt others, second-guess-
ing their thoughts, finishing their sentences, and composing our
responses while they're talking. In doing so, we're dismissing others'
feelings. As Michael Nichols puts it: "Listening means taking in, not
taking over."

I love this quote: "Nobody cares how you much you know
unless they know how much you care." Talking is sharing; listening is caring. When we listen to others, we validate their need to be
acknowledged and understood. All of us want to know we matter.
When we listen to others, we let them know we are trying to understand the world through their eyes. Look around. All around you
there are people simply waiting to be heard. Take the time to listen.

Practice easy-listening the next time someone says, "Can we
talk?" Engage your ears before your mouth.

HAPPINESS HABIT » *Present three special gifts to your spouse, parent,*
or child today: an open mind, an attentive ear, and an understanding heart.

From Rut Dwelling to Risk Taking

Jesus, I want to be a risk-taker, not a safe-player.
Calm my fear and push me! Amen.

YOU CAN'T HELP BUT SMILE AS YOU PASS THIS SIGN ALONG A RURAL HIGHWAY: "Choose Your Rut Carefully...You'll be in it for the next 150 miles."

I challenge you to climb out of your rut, pull yourself upright, and do something courageous. Be a risk-taker; be bold; take a chance; do something different; push back a barrier. And when you're at the end of your rope, tie a knot, hang on, and swing.

Whether it's something as simple as returning to church after a lapse or something as particularly daunting as dating after your marriage ends, take a good look at what's left of your life and choose to make it meaningful.

It's scary to be a risk-taker and to try something new, because we can't help but wonder, "What if I fail?" or "What if I get into this and realize I've made a huge mistake?" Relax. It won't be the first mistake you've made, and no matter how bad, it probably won't be the worst. You gain wisdom, experience, and character by taking risks, even if things don't turn out as planned. You'll be a better person for having tried. Life is full of wonder and surprise. Go for it. Seek it. Never settle for a second-rate life.

HAPPINESS HABIT » *Do something you've been putting off or been hesitant to try. Take a risk. It might be the very thing you need to do.*

PART 4

Reach Out

*"I give you a new commandment:
love one another. As I have loved you,
so you also should love one another.
This is how all will know that
you are my disciples, if you have
love for one another."*

JOHN 13:34–35

Warning: Kindness Can Become Contagious!

*Jesus, all I need to be kind is to get started
and never quit. Amen.*

A S WE MOVED INTO A CIRCLE TO PRAY BEFORE SERVING LUNCH AT OUR LOCAL SOUP KITCHEN, I spotted a dejected woman standing across from me. She stood beside a man whose face radiated sunshine. He turned to her and gave her a big smile. "Thank you," she said. "That smile is better than money."

People often say: "I want to help, but what's there to do?" My response: "Look around." We see abandoned, isolated people everywhere. Let's slow down, look into their eyes, say something kind, and try to make them laugh. Healing-humor is a good pain reliever with no side effects. What about when people tell us to mind our own business? We don't love in order to be loved in return. When Jesus got his hands slapped by his neighbor, he moved on. There's the lesson: We love to love.

When Sheila's baby died, she became a recluse. Two women from my parish with similar experiences determined to bring hope and joy back into her life. They invited Sheila to be their guest at a Josh Groban concert. She resisted. They persisted. Finally, she accepted, and enjoyed herself for the first time in ages. Let's seek out damaged people who are scared, shy, and sad, and give them small doses of kindness. How? Just do it.

HAPPINESS HABIT » *Do something kind this week. Start small and watch your gestures of kindness become contagious.*

Living Unselfishly

Dear Lord, regardless of how small my role,
help me do my part toward easing someone's pain. Amen.

"WELL IT'S JUST MY CROSS TO BEAR," we say while going through illness, disaster, or misery of some kind. We may live with a difficult spouse, work with a cantankerous colleague, grieve a rebellious child, discover nasty rumors about ourselves, or disagree with someone politically, practically, or fundamentally. "It's just my cross to bear."

The cross Jesus asks us to carry involves living in a world unselfishly where other's needs are our priority. Now is a great time to put those needs ahead of our own, starting at home. Read to your child; do the dishes without being asked; play a game with the family; watch a movie together and then talk about it.

Reach out to others by visiting a lonely neighbor or someone in a nursing home or hospital. Those spontaneous acts of caring and comfort can go a long way in easing a burden. A cooked meal, an afternoon chat, an errand run, a gentle hug, a personal note, a phone call—any of these can mean the world to someone in pain.

Living unselfishly means eliminating excuses for not getting involved. This week, choose to give up excuses and take action. There are people waiting for you.

HAPPINESS HABIT » *When your life is ending, you won't remember the moments of success, but rather the moments of filling needs and healing hurts. Reach out. It matters.*

Show Up and Stop

Jesus, as far as you are concerned, I'm somebody who can make a difference in somebody else's life by being kindhearted. Amen.

A FRIEND OF MINE TOLD ME ABOUT A RETIRED DOCTOR WHO CAME TO THE ELEMENTARY SCHOOL WHERE SHE WAS PRINCIPAL. "I'm here to volunteer," he told her. "I can be an aide or a tutor…whatever you need." This doctor became invaluable. His presence taught the entire school community the value of giving without expecting anything in return.

How often have you asked, "What can I do?" without offering any real help? Have you used the excuse, "Sorry, I don't have the time"?

If you want to make a difference, the formula is easy: Show up and stop. Show up for someone who needs you.

This week, begin at home: read a story to your child; help with the dishes without being asked; play a game with the family; watch a movie together and discuss it; visit a hospital patient, a nursing home resident, a lonely neighbor.

Stop worrying about whether you're talented or capable enough. Simply believe you have gifts and abilities waiting to be unwrapped and put to good use. Change comes one person at a time. The next person may just be waiting for you to effect that change.

HAPPINESS HABIT » *Offer to volunteer your time or share your expertise at a non-profit organization in your community this week.*

STALL Snap Judgments

Dear Lord, forgive me for the times I quickly judge others before hearing their story. Amen.

"WHAT DOES SHE SEE IN HIM?" Based on one small thing—someone's weight, their hair, their vocabulary, their accent—we sum up a person, forming snap judgments without even knowing the person. Little to no effort is made to get acquainted or to see whether our initial impression is accurate.

Once you make up your mind about someone, it's difficult to change it. Our judgment often causes that person to react in the same way we are judging them. What's the antidote? STALL.

Stop judging. Be mindful of your thoughts. Notice when a judgment is forming and stop it.

Try walking in their shoes. Converse with them in order to gain an understanding of the circumstances in their life.

Accept them. Once you understand, accept that person for who they are—without trying to change them.

Love them. Even if you don't know them or hated them in the past, love them as a sister or brother, no matter who they are.

Let God be the judge. God sees the whole picture. We don't. Are you up for a challenge? Go for a day, then a week, making judgment-free living part of your routine. Remember: by judging the oyster and dismissing it, we may miss the pearl. Same goes with those we judge.

HAPPINESS HABIT » *Do something special for someone who has been inaccurately judged and dismissed.*

That's What Friends Are For

Jesus, bad things happen in life. I can face them knowing
my friends will be there—especially you! Amen.

A LL AROUND US, FRIENDS ARE CRYING OUT FROM THE PAIN of divorce, sickness, loneliness, unemployment, fears, depression, heartaches, and disappointments. What do we do when we hear their cries? Do we move away? Ignore? Abandon? Or do we move toward them with a comforting presence? How we respond determines the kind of friend we are.

Sometimes, there's very little we can do to fix their problems or change their circumstances. But we can help them by doing what Adele suggests: "Sit in the pain with our friends."

Here's my SOS Plan for Hurting Friends:

Show up. It's important we don't abandon them when they need us most. Be there.

Offer support. Tell them: "I ache with you." "I'll cry with you." "I hurt with you." Then look for practical ways to help, such as taking them dinner, picking up their kids, or walking their dog.

Say little. Just listen without offering advice as they talk it out. Avoid giving them unsolicited solutions to things beyond your control.

We've all been on the hurting side as well as being the shoulder to cry on. Pain lessens when friends rally around to help. Be that friend. Always!

HAPPINESS HABIT » *Reach out to a hurting friend and let them know you're their lifeline.*

Simple Acts

Jesus, I can change a person's whole day just by noticing and paying attention to them. Help me learn to make these small acts of kindness every day. Amen.

"YOUR ORDER'S ALREADY BEEN TAKEN CARE OF," the young clerk said. "The gentleman who was in front of you gave me enough to cover it."

The customer's eyes brimmed with tears. This simple gesture, this random act of kindness, was the encouragement she needed that morning as she picked up the doughnuts to take home to her bedridden husband who was dying of cancer.

Mother Teresa pointed out that the great tragedy of life is not hunger or disease but feeling unnoticed. Everywhere, abandoned, isolated people ache with loneliness. We can hide behind a litany of excuses, like the countless others who swore, "I've got your back" but disappeared when things got tough. Or we can do something.

We don't all have to be like Mother Teresa and travel to remote villages to ease others' pain. You can start with the people sitting across the dinner table from you. Or by standing by someone who's all alone. Reach out to a single mother, a recent widower, a lonely teenager, a rejected friend. They don't need challenges; they need comfort. By simply telling them you're hurting with them, or by touching them with your tears, you'll be sending the message: Somehow, we'll make it through this…together.

HAPPINESS HABIT » *Share the miracle drug—hugging. Show someone you care. Write the letter or card. Make the phone call. Visit the neighbor you've been meaning to see. Your small act of kindness might make someone's day.*

Open Your Eyes

Jesus, someone I'll meet today is lonely and afraid. Give me your words to bring that person comfort, courage, or calm. Amen.

H ELPING OTHERS IS ONE OF THE MOST REWARDING EXPERI-ENCES WE CAN SHARE. In the USA, we cherish the tradition of helping people. Americans are known for our positive, immediate response to those in need. Our telethons and fundraisers bring in countless dollars for Olympic teams, the physically impaired, and victims of hunger and disasters…to name a few. However, these tend to be one-shot deals: We give and then we forget.

Often, we associate giving with money. Certainly, money is important, but is it more valuable than sitting with a dying person who would otherwise be alone? Or delivering a meal to an elderly, housebound individual? Or volunteering to teach reading?

People often say, "I want to help, but what can I do?"

Look around. There are abandoned and isolated people everywhere. Slow down. Look into their eyes. Say something kind. Make them laugh. Healing humor is a great pain reliever…with no side effects!

The Chinese philosopher Lao Tzu wrote, "Kindness in words creates confidence, kindness in thinking creates profoundness, and kindness in giving creates love." Until love is manifested through some caring act, love is nothing more than a very good idea. Open your eyes: The opportunity to show love just might be in your direct line of vision.

HAPPINESS HABIT » *Contact a hurting friend who is having difficulty getting back to normal and let him or her talk. Don't procrastinate— tomorrow may be too late.*

Who Am I?

Jesus, may I never get tired
of saying I love you. Amen.

M OST OF US KNOW THE STORY OF EBENEZER SCROOGE and
his amazing transformation from a hateful, heartless old
man to a cheerful, giving one. That this story is told year after year
suggests the timeless value we hold for a life transformed by love.
Most of us, however, barring the visit of a helpful ghost, will have to
be the architects of love.

Celebrate love as the greatest human virtue, direct from God.
It's the most powerful and potent life-enhancing human energy,
and possibly life's only meaning. Love shows us the way to the most
exciting, full, and wonderful life.

Love is learned and only then does it keep growing. When we
have love in our lives, we're at our most joyous, creative, and capable.
Love brings hope to a lonely person, peace to an upset friend, courage to a fearful relative, and comfort to the homebound. Without
it, lives are empty.

It's time to come together in our need for one another. Embrace
each other with passion and say, "Human person, take my human
hand." Each new moment of love leads to more such moments, and
moment to moment we make this a better world for ourselves and
for all those we encounter.

Be accused of being a hopeless romantic. Be determined not to
die before you discover, develop, and release your potential for love.

HAPPINESS HABIT » *Write love notes and leave them in your child's*
backpack, on your spouse's computer monitor, or your friend's windshield.

The Hurry-It-Up Generation

Jesus, I've gotten used to getting things right away.
Give me an extra dose of patience to wait. Amen.

"ALEXA. I NEED AN ANSWER *NOW*." And you get it. We're the "hurry-it-up generation" who wants, and expects, everything now. Waiting isn't an option. There are movies on demand and instant messaging—conveniences in life that require little-to-no patience.

Hurry-it-up dictates our lives. Drivers honk because traffic is moving too slowly. Foot tapping accompanies the wait as the computer reboots. Frustration increases as an elderly parent repeats the same story again. If we allow it, impatience can ruin our lives, as stress, anxiety, and irritation become regular house guests.

You need to stop and ask *who*, *what*, and *how* to effectively manage impatience. *Who* is testing your patience? A friend who is always late? *What* situations get the best of you?

Slow-moving lines at the grocery store? Promises not fulfilled according to your timetable? *What* circumstances are beyond your control? Rather than giving them over to anxiety or annoyance, let them go.

How do you change the circumstances that try your patience? Reach out to the person who triggers it. Frame your comments with "When you_____, I feel _____." Listen as they respond and work together on positive changes.

"Only God has perfect timing; never early, never late. It takes a little patience, but it's worth the wait..." -Anonymous

HAPPINESS HABIT » *Identify your impatience triggers.*
How do you feel right before you lose it?

Be a Seize-the-Moment Responder

Jesus, a kindness done is never lost or forgotten by you. Amen.

A S WENDY STOOD WAITING FOR THE TRAFFIC LIGHT TO CHANGE, she noticed a teenager standing on the opposite curb, crying. When the light changed, they started crossing the street toward each other. Just as they were about to pass, Wendy's motherly instincts kicked in, but she stifled the urge to reach out and comfort the girl, and she kept walking.

Days later, the girl's tear-filled eyes still haunted Wendy. "Why didn't I ask her if she needed help?" she asked me. "Only a few seconds would have been enough to let her know someone cared. Instead, I acted as if she didn't exist."

Often, our own problems keep us from helping others in pain. Other times, we're afraid we might say the wrong thing and make matters worse. We need to become "seize-the-moment" responders.

A "seize-the-moment" responder is alert—noticing the distant teenager, the preoccupied spouse, or the distracted coworker—and drops everything to spend time with the person in need.

Be available when an adult child stops by needing to talk. Turn off your phone and listen. When a timid soul comes looking for praise, pile it on. When a sad friend needs a hug, give them one. Be there when you're needed. After all, God doesn't take away our crosses. He simply sends other Christians to help us carry them.

HAPPINESS HABIT » *Express your thanks to the people who stayed with you when you felt overworked, overdrawn, or overlooked.*

Little Things Do Matter

*Jesus, I want my kindness to have a ripple effect and spread
to lift up others who need a dose of encouragement today. Amen.*

MY FRIEND LIKES TO SURPRISE HER COWORKERS WITH SMALL GIFTS AND NOTES to let them know they matter. "It isn't much," she says, "a candy bar, cookie, or flower. I have fun letting them know they're special."

With generous hearts and willing hands, we can make a difference. Many of us would like to impact people's lives by alleviating some pain or giving a boost of happiness. Each of us can do just that in simple ways: a pat on the back, an enthusiastic high-five, a smile, an open door, a kiss on the cheek, a nod of the head, or a thank-you note to a friend.

These simple actions poke holes in someone else's darkness, allowing the light to filter in and heal wounds, build bridges, and provide comfort. We may never know how our aptly timed actions have touched and changed lives with hope and encouragement. Once we touch the life of just one person, they're likely to go and do the same for someone else.

HAPPINESS HABIT » *Write notes of encouragement to your family and friends today. Share special quotes, poems, or Bible verses. Then leave them on pillows, bulletin boards, or in lunch boxes or backpacks. Boost their confidence by letting them know they matter.*

PART 5

Practice Forgiveness

"And be kind to one another, compassionate, forgiving one another as God has forgiven you in Christ."

EPHESIANS 4:32

Burying the Proverbial Hatchet

*Jesus, help me to use forgiveness to call a truce
in my embattled relationships. Amen.*

FORGIVING PEOPLE WHEN THEY APOLOGIZE IS ONE THING, but have you ever tried to forgive someone who has hurt you and never shown any remorse? Not so easy, is it? It's tough to bury that hatchet.

Even after years spent developing a relationship, a single harsh statement or thoughtless act can destroy everything we feel for that person. We forget the good and play out bitter, vindictive scenarios in our minds.

When someone hurts us, we have choices. We can go our separate ways and never talk again. We can live with the anger. We can bear grudges, nurse hate, or seek revenge. We can pretend everything is fine and just bury our feelings. Or we can face the person and talk things through…and then forgive.

You guessed it: the last choice is the healthy one. Even if the person who wronged you refuses to change or take responsibility, you can still let go of pride and bring closure and healing—for your own sake.

Of course, forgetting is the hardest part of forgiving. We bury the hatchet; but when we leave the handle sticking out of the ground, we're just giving the pain permission to continue cutting us. Bury the handle. Cancel the debt.

That's the only way to experience true freedom.

HAPPINESS HABIT » *Wash the slate clean. Get yourself a wipe-off board. List the names of those you have hurt and how you hurt them. Write an "I'm washing my slate clean" letter to all the people you hurt. Then wipe their names off the board.*

Favor Yourself

Jesus, I will rush to forgive anyone who has offended me,
because I know the precious value of time. Amen.

H AVE YOU HEARD OF THE LITTLE BOY WHO PRAYED, "Father forgive us our trespasses, as we give it to those who trespass against us"? When told to forgive, we think we're being asked to do something for someone who doesn't deserve it. It's not easy, because we think of the offense. Why should we let them off the hook?

Often, we want to lash back instead of forgiving. Lewis Smedes writes, "Forgiveness is spiritual surgery. You slice out your past damage that shouldn't be there." When we refuse, it comes back to us. I call this the "boomerang effect." When we throw out revenge, harsh words, or nastiness, they all return to us.

Do yourself a favor—forgive. When harsh words are exchanged and relationships harmed, settle the wrong and heal the hurt. Surrender your right to get even.

Remember, forgiveness isn't about them; it's about us. When we choose to rub it out, rather than rubbing it in, we can have peace in our lives.

HAPPINESS HABIT » *Pray: "Compassionate God, I choose to forgive (name the person) for (what they did) even though I feel (share the painful feelings). Gentle God, I choose not to hold any grudges against (name) any longer. Thank you for freeing me from my hatred. Keep us both safe in your love. Amen."*

Turn Hate Upside Down

Jesus, when you were hurt again and again by those you loved,
you continued to pursue them, love them, and seek the best for them.
Help me model your example. Amen.

"I DON'T LOVE YOU ANYMORE. I WANT A DIVORCE." The words cut deeply.

"I've had it. Please don't call me again." Your friend's words seem unfair.

"The bulk of the estate has been left to your brother." After all you've done, now your absentee brother reaps the rewards.

Hurt. Anger. Disappointment. What do you do? Love them. What?

Love them. It may not be easy, but it's exactly what Jesus wants you to do.

Difficult? Most assuredly. But not impossible. Take comfort in knowing that you aren't alone. The people of Jesus' day didn't know what to do with Jesus' "love your enemies" commandment, either. "Turn the other cheek" and "love those who hate you" are radical teachings. But they're your ticket out of hate, fear, and chaos.

That rug under which you often sweep your feelings of hurt and disappointment will eventually end up being a nearly insurmountable heap of ugliness. Stop it! It may be a tall order to love your enemies—but nothing will bring you more peace.

HAPPINESS HABIT » *Journal around these questions: How do I really love someone who is hurtful? Do I allow this person to stay in my life, or should I shut him/her out, to protect myself from further hurt? Is there something I can say or do to resolve the situation?*

Forgiveness Cures

Jesus, after I bury my painful past,
please give me long-term amnesia. Amen.

"H E STILL HAUNTS MY LIFE," THE WOMAN SAID, angry eyes fresh with tears. "I hate him! It doesn't make me feel any better that he's in jail. He deserves to die! I will never forgive him."

Have you ever felt this way? Physical or emotional abuse creates deep wounds. Human nature demands justice—sweet revenge.

We feel that justice is accomplished when we hurt those who have hurt us, disappoint those who have let us down, inflict suffering on those who have caused us pain. We think the slate will only be wiped clean when they experience our revenge.

A close relationship that may have brought us much joy is gone because of one rude comment, an insensitive act, or a cutting criticism. But our idea of justice is not the answer! Forgiveness is. But forgiveness comes hard, and we fail to realize that when we choose to hold on to our pain, we carry around the useless burden of hatred and sorrow, which weighs us down—while having no effect on the one who has hurt us.

Harboring hatred and seeking retribution lead us nowhere. Only by letting go of the hatred and the need for revenge can we find our way to the cure—forgiveness. We're human and imperfect, but we forgive anyway. Why? Because the price we pay for not forgiving is much too great.

HAPPINESS HABIT » *If you're carrying around unforgiveness, try speaking these words over and over: "I forgive (person's name)." Don't stop until you get the message.*

Care, Confront, and Come Clean

Jesus, I know my friend's actions were not intended to cause harm. Give me the words to confront lovingly so we will find healing and peace. Amen.

B EING LOVINGLY TRUTHFUL WITH SOMEONE WHO HAS WRONGED US TAKES TWO ABILITIES: wisdom to know when to speak and when to keep quiet, and courage to face the outcome of the confrontation. Sometimes our best efforts to show love and reconciliation are met with the worst expressions of anger and denial. Pray for guidance and try to be patient. Consider these four steps to mend the relationship:

> *Confidentially Confront:* Avoid sharing the issue with uninvolved people.

> *Come Clean:* Tell the truth. Don't hold back.

> *Continue Caring:* Say, "We need to talk" when problems develop. Your words will be softer and your message more clearly heard.

> *Contact Help:* If you still experience the same negative behavior, get in touch with a priest or counselor, so both sides are heard and weighed by a third party.

When Jesus talked about loving confrontation, his words applied to serious situations, not petty issues. Choose your battles. Know your boundaries. When the wrongdoer won't acknowledge that some change is required, get on with your own life.

HAPPINESS HABIT » *Is there someone with whom you have an unresolved confrontation? Send that person a text or email message: "Our friendship is valuable to me. Can we can resolve our issues?" Take the first step, then follow through with the four steps listed above.*

From Response to Repair

Jesus, repair me slowly and gently, but heal me. Amen.

"I SCREAMED AND CALLED ASHLEY ALL KINDS OF NAMES," Patrick confessed after discovering his wife's infidelity with her old boyfriend. "She just sat there for an hour and listened."

Betrayal conjures up powerful and painful emotions. It's one thing to be disappointed in someone we love and trust, but to feel violated—betrayed—is another thing altogether. Jesus knew all about betrayal, from Judas cashing in and checking out, to Peter's flat-out denial.

Betrayal victims go through an emotional process:

Response: This is a bad dream. I'm going to wake up and everything will be fine.

Retreat: People turn on you and let you down.

Regret: I was warned. I should have listened.

Rage: I'm so angry, I could…

Revenge: One day they'll pay for what they did to me. I'll get them.

Repair: I want to be free from this pain and not let it change me into someone I don't like.

Choosing to continue in a relationship after the painful trauma of betrayal requires more than a simple apology or promise that it won't happen again. It takes a soft heart along with plenty of talk and time.

HAPPINESS HABIT » *When betrayed and working on recovery, wake up each morning and say: "It wasn't my fault. I choose to trust again."*

Got Forgiveness?

Jesus, help me make peace with what is, redirect my energy,
and then allow forgiveness to rule my heart. Amen.

M OST OF US HAVE ONE THING IN COMMON: we've been hurt by someone we love. It may have happened years ago or just yesterday. It may have been subtle or overwhelming, but whatever the intensity, we've not forgotten it and still carry its scars.

I've met hundreds of people who harbor past hurts. They stay tied up in knots because they refuse to forgive. These rifts in relationships are so great that some people never speak to each other again. It may be difficult to forgive, but when we continue to suffer from these hurtful feelings, we give our power away. We have to work to change these feelings. It's a journey, and it's a choice. If we continue to hold grudges, we are only damaging ourselves. It's likely that the person who hurt us has moved on. Can we move on? Can we choose to feel differently?

Forgiving is not about approving the hurtful behavior; it's about healing the memory so it no longer rules our lives. We can do that by redirecting our focus and our energy by doing something for ourselves every day that helps us to feel better about our lives.

HAPPINESS HABIT » *Forgiving those who hurt us is not a one-shot deal. It's a journey and it begins with a choice. God gives us a certain amount of energy to spend each day, and only we can decide how to use it. Spend your energy today by offering forgiveness and letting go of the hurt.*

Getting on the Same Side of the Fence

Jesus, I don't want to be stubborn.
Help me to see another's point of view. Amen.

I SIT WITH PEOPLE WHO ARE TORN BY MISUNDERSTANDING. They long to be close to one another but are separated by a huge chasm of disagreement, hurt feelings, or resentment. Whether it's with your spouse or a best friend, there will inevitably be moments of misunderstanding.

Until you learn to resolve them, they metastasize, becoming cancerous to the relationship. To avoid perpetual conflict, you must come to an agreement.

Don't ignore it; iron out the problem by practicing the three Rs: relinquish, resist, and refocus. Forget "my way" or "your way" thinking. You need to focus on "our way." *Relinquish* your need to always be right. *Resist* criticizing, yelling, name-calling, or forcing your opinion on the other person. Do not dismiss their point of view; that will only add fuel to the fire. Finally, *refocus* by putting yourself in the other person's shoes and seeing the issue through their eyes.

This different approach is important in gaining understanding rather than figuring out who's right and who's wrong. By honoring the other person's opinion, it eases tension, opens the door to permanent solutions, and helps you move forward together harmoniously.

HAPPINESS HABIT » *How do you typically deal with misunderstanding in your relationships? Is it effective? If not, try the three Rs: relinquish, resist, and refocus.*

No Budge on a Grudge

Jesus, it hurts me to be unforgiving.
Free me from the prison of myself. Amen.

UNKIND WORDS. BROKEN VOWS. ABSENT PARENTS. UNAPPRECIATIVE CHILDREN. I meet many people consumed by bitterness and resentment. They harbor unresolved hurts from the past that affect their present. They refuse to forgive and move on.

When we've been hurt, we often strike back rather than strengthen and heal valuable relationships. Finding it difficult to let bygones be bygones, we refuse to bury the hatchet. Essentially, we live with revenge and hatred, with grudges running deep and lasting a lifetime.

All of us experience injuries that defy explanation. But postponing forgiveness deprives us of wholesome living. If we don't practice forgiveness, we often end up being the ones who suffer the most. While we shouldn't minimize the wrong or deny the other person's responsibility for hurting us, we do need to let go of the grudge so our lives will no longer be defined by how we've been hurt.

Forgiveness is more about how we change than about how the other person reacts. When we refuse to let the offenses take up permanent residence in our lives, we prevent the wounds from festering, and we can move toward healing, peace, and happiness.

HAPPINESS HABIT » *Reflect on Sidney Simon's words: "Forgiveness is freeing up and putting to better use the energy once consumed by holding grudges, harboring resentments, and nursing unhealed wounds."*

The Remedy Is in the Writing

Jesus, I was wronged. I want to wipe the slate clean,
but I need your help to choose forgiveness. Amen.

WHEN WAS THE LAST TIME YOU THOUGHT ABOUT "THAT PERSON"? You know, the one who betrayed you. When we pick at a wound, it never heals. It's our choice to live in the land of denial or to seek payback by getting even. When we choose the latter, it's usually a lose-lose game. However, when we choose the hardest option—forgiveness—we can welcome peace back into our lives.

Real forgiveness requires an acknowledgment of the pain. When pain is undeserved, it hurts all the more. At the same time, hostility, and even hatred, tends to creep in. Drain the pain. Get angry. Scream into a pillow. Cry. Allow yourself to feel sad. Bottling up emotions can make the process of forgiveness much harder. Don't be afraid to feel what you feel.

As the pain drains, don't excuse the person's actions. But try to understand their motivations. As the pain dwindles, dump it so the memories of what happened no longer haunt you. Forgiveness is a lifestyle change of the heart. It frees us so we no longer feel imprisoned and owned by the person who hurt us.

Forgiveness gently soothes us as the burning coals of revenge and resentment slowly, but surely, cool within.

HAPPINESS HABIT » *List the people who make you angry or resentful. Write each one a letter. Mail the letters or dispose of them. The remedy of forgiveness is in the writing.*

Resolve to Reconcile

Dear God, you understand the sorrow of unfinished business.
Help me work through mine so I that I may find peace again. Amen.

C AROLINE CAME TO SEE ME THREE WEEKS AFTER HER FATHER DIED OF A HEART ATTACK. She was away when it happened and was devastated by the news. They had a heated argument two days before he died, and harsh words had been spoken. She was regretful for things said and unsaid. "What did you argue about? I asked. "Something stupid," she replied.

Unfinished business can be major, such as a bitter rivalry among siblings, family secrets that were never shared, or important matters that remain unresolved. It could be a child who has not spoken to his or her parents in years, a spouse who dies suddenly during a crisis, or a last will and testament that was never completed.

More often, less dramatic events cause misunderstandings: A mother may still feel guilty about punishing her daughter, a wife may not have forgiven her husband, or a son may believe that his parents loved his brother more. In Caroline's case, a daughter was disappointed that her father died before they could be reconciled. These memories can be overwhelming for the person left to grieve.

Unfinished business deprives us of a sense of peace. It seems final. We've lost our last chance to work through old issues or to tell someone how we really feel.

HAPPINESS HABIT » *If you still live with haunting memories, nagging resentments or even anger, consider talking to a trusted friend, priest, or grief counselor so you can process your feelings. Seek to gain closure. Talk it out. Don't leave things unsaid that need to be said. Resolve to reconcile with your past so you can move on with your life.*

Grow
in Faith

"You planted them;
they have taken root,
they flourish
and bear fruit as well."

JEREMIAH 12:2

Me? No Way!

Jesus, as you continually fashion and form me into the person I ought to be, open my ears to hear your gentle voice whisper, "Follow me." Amen.

MICHELANGELO STOOD CHISELING A HUGE, UNSIGHTLY PIECE OF GRANITE. A passerby said, "What are you doing?" He said, "I see an angel trapped in this rock, and I'm letting the angel out."

Have you wondered if you can ever be set free from the person you became? Although you may have made a thousand mistakes and feel like that old, rough rock, Jesus looks at you and says, "I see in you an angel, a child of God. Somebody I can use." As he helps remove the parts that aren't "angel," Jesus chips away at your life. It hurts, yes, but he must bring out the person trapped inside the rock. Jesus wants to set you free from the thoughtless and often cruel remarks of others.

When the world saw Jesus' disciples, they saw rough, smelly fishermen, despised tax collectors, and fanatical politicians. But Jesus saw people who could turn the world upside down with the gospel.

Jesus said, "You are Simon, but you shall be Peter." Don't worry about what you are—think about what you shall be: a unique and special person. My value lies in the fact that I am me, and yours in the fact that you are you. If we were all the same, there would be no surprises, laughter, or creativity. Take comfort: there will always be people who accept you.

People often say to me, "Thanks for being you." My answer is, "I tried for years to be someone else. It didn't work."

HAPPINESS HABIT » *This week, seek out scared, sad, and shy people. Give them some inspiration—a quote, story, poem, or Bible passage— to ignite their spirits. Help set them free to believe in themselves. And for you: look in a mirror and say three positive things about yourself. Honor yourself with dignity and respect.*

A Life-Sustaining Rule

Jesus, I want to always treat others right. I know my actions can boomerang back on me, instantly. Amen.

"LET US REMEMBER THE GOLDEN RULE: DO UNTO OTHERS"—Pope Francis's words to the Congress of the United States were interrupted by a rousing standing ovation—"as you would have them do unto you." Despite the simplicity of the message, these words challenge us to go beyond simply being pleasant or going out of our way to be helpful. They require us to think about others, including those who may be quite different from us, and to consider how they might think and feel.

Living the Golden Rule is as important as breathing. It is like life-sustaining air, food, and water. It's recognizing that everyone, as individuals with their own opinions and feelings, deserves respect and consideration. By practicing the Golden Rule, we show empathy, compassion, kindness, and respect as we reach out a helping hand, listen without judgment, and keep our critical tongue in check.

It's easy to brush off the Golden Rule as if it's meant for someone else. But in reality, it isn't difficult to be kind and gracious to all. After a bit of practice, it starts to feel natural and you begin to recognize its powers.

HAPPINESS HABIT » *Practice the Golden Rule by starting small. Be cheerful in your interactions with the people you encounter throughout your day.*

Remember Who You Are

*Dear Lord, sometimes I remember what I should
forget—failures, struggles, or hurts caused by others.
Help me not to dwell on them. Amen.*

S OMETIMES, ON MY FREQUENT VISITS TO NORMAN, HE WOULD
KNOW MY NAME. Other times, he wouldn't. Eventually, he even
forgot his own name. At the end, his body began to shut down. It's as
if his lungs forgot to breathe and his heart forgot to beat. Alzheimer's
is like that. When Simba (*The Lion King*, 1994) runs with a different
crowd, he loses his way. When he looks in the water, his reflection is the
face of his father, Mufasa, reminding him, "Remember who you are."

Teenagers often need that same reminder. So do we. The moment
we catch spiritual amnesia and forget our intrinsic God-given signif-
icance, we take a step backwards, opening ourselves up to all kinds
of self-defeating behaviors. We say or do harmful things before real-
izing, "That's not who I am."

Today, remember you are a holy, unrepeatable masterpiece of
God. You came into this world fully loaded and equipped—one of
a kind, an original. Your uniqueness influences everything you do.
Whatever challenges or difficulties life throws your way, know that
you have the care and protection of the One who created you. Never
forget that.

HAPPINESS HABIT » *Complete this sentence: "I am…" with only
positive, life-affirming words. Remember this sentence whenever you feel
down.*

Simplify! Simplify!

Jesus, sometimes my stuff holds me back from looking deeply into what is important in my life. I'm going to take stock, downsize, and keep it simple. Amen.

I OFTEN HEAR AFFLUENT PEOPLE RECALL THE EARLY DAYS, when they had little of monetary value: a one-room apartment, an old car, a slim bank balance. Yet they refer to those days as among the happiest they've ever known. Still, we don't tend to strive for the simple lives we claim to want, assuming that accumulating things is better.

Defining ourselves by the number of things we have, we fail to recognize that the more we own, the more we are possessed by what we own. It's well to remember that there are no moving vans or armored trucks in a funeral procession!

One day, while watching a little girl flying a kite in a park, I noticed she was totally caught up in the moment, mesmerized by the gentle movements of her kite. There she was, close to home, with a few sticks, paper, string, a little wind, and a great stretch of sky—pure simplicity.

Life is simple. By downsizing, we can enjoy the simple pleasures—a sunrise, fall colors, the taste of food, laughing at a child's joke, sandcastles, freshly fallen snow, intimate conversation, breakfast in bed, a good book, a blooming crocus. When the clutter threatens to possess us, keep in mind the words of Henry David Thoreau, "Simplify! Simplify!"

HAPPINESS HABIT » *When you purchase a new item such as a new shirt or mug, remove two items and donate them to a local shelter or vintage clothing store.*

Keep Pedaling

Jesus, you're always there to push, pull,
or drag me through my mistake slump. Amen.

ARE YOU SITTING ON THE SIDELINES OF LIFE FEELING WASHED UP? Have you made mistakes and experienced setbacks and feel as if you don't have much of a future? I hear it all the time. I have an addiction. I ruined my marriage. I failed in business. A negative past doesn't make it impossible for you to have a bright future. No mistake is too much for God's compassionate mercy. If we continue to crucify ourselves, however, it will prevent us from receiving the good things God wants for us.

If we spend our time focusing on our mistakes, they can cripple us, causing us to cut our dreams short. I didn't finish college. I didn't spend enough time with my family. I took my spouse for granted. When we veer off course, God doesn't tell us "you blew it." Rather, God has a recovery plan for us—POA (Pedal On Attitude). He's cheering us on to keep on pedaling, so we can learn, adjust, grow, and improve. God is a God of another chance. You are not defined by your mistakes. Let them go. Be your best today...and pedal on!

HAPPINESS HABIT » *Write on an index card an inspirational quote about moving past mistakes. On the other side, share a personal support prayer. Give it to someone who is living with regrets. POA—Pass it on!*

Face the Unexpected with Faith

Jesus, you have given me two hands—one for receiving help and the other for giving help. Show me the way to use both hands. Amen.

EVERYTHING WAS GOING FINE FOR MARY AND JOSEPH—THEY WERE IN LOVE. They looked forward to getting married and raising a family. Surprise! God had a different plan.

Life's surprises will always catch us off guard. The only way to turn is toward faith and faces:

Faith: When we're hit with the unexpected, we must believe God is big enough to take care of us. We must ask God to give us what we need. He won't disappoint us.

Faces: We don't have the strength to survive alone. We need faces that are touchable, approachable, available. We want a place to cry, a person to care, the security of friends who will share our hurt. Shared joy is double joy. Shared sorrow is half a sorrow.

It's easy to collapse when we're hit with the unexpected. Yet if we do, we might find ourselves near the end of our lives thinking, "If I'd had more faith in God, what might I have done? If I'd reached out further, what might I have become?"

HAPPINESS HABIT » *Give up a favorite activity and use the time to talk with a friend or neighbor who could use some propping up.*

God's Unique Creation

Jesus, when I'm quiet, I can hear your gentle voice whisper,
"You're special." Thank you for never giving up on me. Amen.

I LOVE ME. Even with all my frailties, my capacity to hurt, forget, cause conflict, and feel fear, I'm delighted with myself. Self-discovery is an exciting journey. Take the time to find out who you are. I promise you, you'll not be disappointed.

Believe that you, and you alone, control your destiny. You can be what you want to be—but not until you stop listening to the put-downs, criticisms, and comparisons.

I love life. Life is always open and ready to share its resources. It simply waits for our embrace, offering us choices, approving our decisions, and walking toward us. Life is continuously forgiving, amazingly adjustable, always accepting, and forever encouraging. It doesn't hold us irrevocably bound to our past but willingly offers us a fresh start with each new moment. Each dawn brings with it a never-been-seen-or-lived-before kind of day. The tree outside your window is never the same—so look at it! There have never been two sunsets exactly the same since the beginning of time—so look!

In the end, we must each live our own life; no one else can live it for us. Choose to love...yourself and your life.

HAPPINESS HABIT » *Write a thank-you note to someone who has been a positive influence in your life. Better yet: Call that person and take him/her out to lunch. Oh, and look in the mirror (before you're made up or dressed up) and smile. Do it every day...and before you go to bed.*

Confess the Mess

Jesus, help me to believe my mess-ups are never final; instead,
they are opportunities to fess up and do better next time. Amen.

O KAY, SO YOU'VE MESSED UP. So what? I've messed up and will again. I tried to be super mature in my own strength and fell flat on my face. At other times I went to the opposite extreme, waiting for God to make me super mature without me making an effort. Again, I fell flat on my face.

When I do mess up, I fess up to a few close friends. Their empathy, love, and vulnerability encourage and strengthen me. So does their forgiveness when I admit my mistakes. It's a conversion to open our eyes, admit our blunders, and accept full responsibility.

Jesus was a fess-up friend; no wonder he had so many dinner invitations. Being with him changed people's lives. Jesus helped people see and accept their human imperfections, giving them room to admit their mistakes and strength to meet frustration and failure. Fessing up makes us accountable.

This is an essential component of our spiritual and emotional growth. We're always growing, gaining insights, and learning from our daily experiences. Our mess-ups can be some of life's greatest teachers—if we choose to learn from them rather than let them crush us. What have your mess-ups taught you?

HAPPINESS HABIT » *Consider finding your own fess-up friend.*
Select this person from among people who know you the best—your spouse,
pastor, or close friends.

The Reward of Discomfort

*Jesus, I can only walk on water by stepping out of the boat
and trusting you to be there. Amen.*

IN *LEAD WITH HUMILITY*, JEFFREY KRAMES ILLUSTRATES HOW POPE FRANCIS HAS BREATHED LIFE INTO AN AGING INSTITU-TION, energized a global base, and created real hope for the future. Reflecting on the pope's humility, the author offers twelve simple principles we can use for effective leadership. My favorite is: "Shake up the status quo and get out of your comfort zone."

Comfort zones are familiar and predictable. Nothing changes. But at what cost? We're held hostage to boredom and fear, trapped in the "I'm stuck" syndrome, hiding behind our I've-always-done-it-this-way excuses.

Now is the time to stretch those limits. Start small. Switch up your daily routine. Head to bed early and wake with the sun. Change your pew at church. Try a new restaurant.

When an opportunity, promotion, or challenge presents itself, think tall and go for it! Don't allow naysayers to pace in your head, trapping you in your comfort zone. Hit the mute button and ignore their words: "You can't!" "You're not good enough!" "You'll fail!" Rather, tune into your personal pep squad: "Give it a try!" "You're capable!"

It takes a conscious effort to push ourselves beyond our comfort zones. But when we do, we can enjoy spiritual, emotional, and financial growth.

HAPPINESS HABIT » *Leaving your comfort zone can be as simple as moving to a new apartment or taking on a new volunteer opportunity. You never know what is around the next corner!*

The Clock Is Ticking

Jesus, you call yourself "I Am," not "I Was," or "I'm Gonna Be."
Help me to live in the precious present always. Amen.

W E ALL HAVE HAD MOMENTS IN LIFE THAT WE WISH WOULD LAST FOREVER. Unfortunately, life doesn't happen that way. Unless we celebrate and enjoy them as they happen, we may miss their impact on our lives, for sooner than we'd like, they are gone. Alan told me, "Since I have cancer, my wife and I have forgotten the meaning of tomorrow. When one of us says, 'Let's…,' the other says, 'Yes!' before the sentence is finished."

Nothing lasts forever in this world. We only have the present, the now. The past is gone. Even though it seems ever so close, the future is always out of our reach. We can dream about it, but it is untouchable until it becomes the present. When we live in the present, we're living where life unfolds. The past was, and the future will be, but the present is all there is right now.

Most of us forget that we have a limited amount of time on earth. But the time to make the phone call is now. It's time to say, "You're important to me. Even though I seem to forget, I don't. My life would be empty without you."

Value every moment as if it were your last. Don't just talk about it. Live it!

HAPPINESS HABIT » *Have the conversation with those you love now. The clock is ticking. Make the most of it.*

Also by Fr. Joseph F. Sica

FORGIVENESS
ONE STEP *at a* TIME

"In this gentle gem, Father Joe admirably blends real-life stories, down-to-earth wisdom, and sparkling wit to make forgiveness as important and as necessary as breathing. This is, by far, the book to read for those who are struggling to move beyond their feelings of anger and revenge to forgiveness. It will change lives."

SISTER HELEN PREJEAN,
author of Dead Man Walking

As Christians we are challenged to embrace forgiveness, one of the most difficult Christian virtues. Here Father Joe Sica offers ten invaluable steps to help you take forgiveness seriously: handling injury; getting stuck in the past; wanting payback; telling everybody about it; waking up; loving confrontation; setting boundaries; patching up; reaping benefits; and moving on. He calls these "dance steps" and has choreographed them beautifully to connect with Jesus' teaching about forgiveness. Each step includes something to learn (path), something to consider (ponder), something to do (practice), and something to say (prayer).

Father Joe's stories and anecdotes give life to his message and illustrate the inner peace and freedom that true forgiveness brings.

152 PAGES | $12.95 | 5½" x 8½" | 9781585957620

TO ORDER CALL 1-800-321-0411 | **TWENTY-THIRD PUBLICATIONS**
OR VISIT WWW.TWENTYTHIRDPUBLICATIONS.COM | A division of Bayard, Inc.